For Kate Brigmon—D.D.M.

For my family, who supported me doing what I love—C.G.

13 12 11 10 09 08 07 06   9 8 7 6 5 4 3 2 1

Library of Congress Cataloging-in-Publication Data

Mackall, Dandi Daley.
God shows the way / written by Dandi Daley Mackall ; pictures by Claudine Gévry.
p. cm. -- (My favorite verses)
ISBN 0-7847-1821-0 (casebound picture book)
1. Ten commandments--Juvenile literature.
I. Gévry, Claudine. II. Title. III. Series: Mackall, Dandi Daley. My favorite verses.

BV4656.M33 2006   222'.160520834--dc22   2006000025

MY FAVORITE VERSES

With ten rules to obey,

GOD SHOWS THE WAY

Written by
Dandi Daley Mackall

Pictures by
Claudine Gévry

Standard®
PUBLISHING
Bringing The Word to Life

Cincinnati, Ohio

I don't always do all the things that I should.
As much as I want to, it's hard to be good.

But God knew the problem and gave me a guide—

ten rules I can follow
with God by my side.

Then God instructed the people as follows: I am the LORD your God, who rescued you.

Exodus 20:1, 2

There's only one God, and we only need one.
He made the whole world. Then he gave us his Son!

I know that
there's only one God.

RULE #1   Do not worship any other gods besides me.

Exodus 20:3

I really like sand castles, ice cream, and swings.
But God is much better than all of those things!

I promise to love
my God best.

Do not make idols of any kind.

Exodus 20:4

I'll never say "God" when I'm feeling upset.
For God's name is holy—I shouldn't forget.

I promise to honor God's name.

RULE #3   Do not misuse the name of the LORD.

Exodus 20:7

Make Sunday a holy day—that's not so tough.
For other stuff, six days are surely enough!

I'll keep Sunday
especially for God.

RULE #4   Remember to observe the Sabbath day by keeping it holy.

Exodus 20:8

Since God says to honor my mom and my dad,
I won't talk all sassy or stay fuming mad.

I'll do what my mom
and dad say.

RULE #5   Honor your father and mother.

Exodus 20:12

God says, "Don't kill!" So I won't even hate.

I'll celebrate life because life is so great!

I'll value the life
that God gives.

RULE #6   Do not murder.

Exodus 20:13

I guess I might marry, but I don't know who.
I'll always be faithful, 'cause God tells me to.

I'll honor the person I love.

RULE #7   Do not commit adultery.

Exodus 20:14

I might see a toy that I think is ideal.
Still, I wouldn't take it,
'cause God says, "Don't steal."

I won't take those things
that aren't mine.

RULE #8   Do not steal.

Exodus 20:15

I don't want to gossip—that wouldn't be wise.
Why should I hurt someone's feelings with lies?

I promise that
I'll tell the truth.

RULE #9   Do not testify falsely against your neighbor.

Exodus 20:16

If I've got one cat,
but my buddy has nine . . .

Instead of complaining, I'll thank God for mine.

I won't be all jealous
or mad!

RULE #10   Do not covet...anything else your neighbor owns.

Exodus 20:17

God wrote these ten rules on a tablet of stone.
I never could keep them if I were alone.

But God gave me Jesus
to show me the way,
and sent me his Spirit
to help me obey.

I am the LORD your God, who rescued you.

Exodus 20:2

Exodus 20:1-17

¹Then God instructed the people as follows:
²"I am the LORD your God, who rescued you from slavery in Egypt.

³"Do not worship any other gods besides me.

⁴"Do not make idols of any kind, whether in the shape of birds or animals or fish. ⁵You must never worship or bow down to them, for I, the LORD your God, am a jealous God who will not share your affection with any other god! . . . ⁶But I lavish my love on those who love me and obey my commands, even for a thousand generations.

⁷"Do not misuse the name of the LORD your God. The LORD will not let you go unpunished if you misuse his name.

⁸"Remember to observe the Sabbath day by keeping it holy. ⁹Six days a week are set apart for your daily duties and regular work, ¹⁰but the seventh day is a day of rest dedicated to the LORD your God. On that day no one in your household may do any kind of work. . . . ¹¹For in six days

the LORD made the heavens, the earth, the sea, and everything in them; then he rested on the seventh day. That is why the LORD blessed the Sabbath day and set it apart as holy.

12 "Honor your father and mother.
Then you will live a long, full life in the land the LORD your God will give you.

13 "Do not murder.

14 "Do not commit adultery.

15 "Do not steal.

16 "Do not testify falsely against your neighbor.

17 "Do not covet your neighbor's house.
. . . or anything else your neighbor owns."